The Dog Lover's Guide

FULL OF USEFUL TIPS and lots of tricks!

The Dog Lover's Guide

FULL OF USEFUL TIPS and lots of tricks!

By Honor Head

QED

QED Publishing

Editorial Director: Victoria Garrard
Art Director: Laura Roberts-Jensen
QED Designer: Rosie Levine

Designed by Poppy Joslin and Starry Dog Books Ltd.
Edited and picture researched by Starry Dog Books Ltd.

First published in the UK in 2014 by
QED Publishing
A Quarto Group company
The Old Brewery,
6 Blundell Street,
London,
N7 9BH

www.qed-publishing.co.uk

A catalogue record for this book is available from the British Library.

ISBN 978-1-78171-917-6

Printed in China

Words in **bold** are
explained in the
glossary on page 112.

Contents

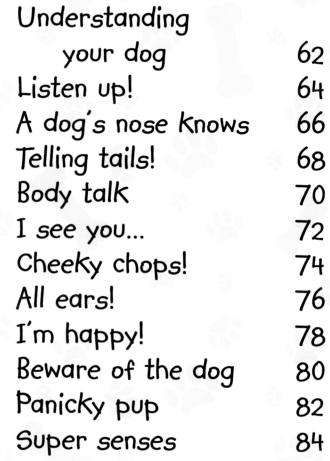

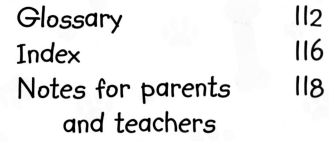

4 TRAINING & TRICKS 86

This dog is having a check-up at the vet's.

"What do you think of my topknot?"

Make bath time fun for your dog.

1

DOG CARE

There's more to looking after a dog than just walks and feeding. If it becomes ill, you must take it to the **vet**, and some dogs need to be bathed and brushed a lot. But if you look after your dog, you will have a happy, healthy pet full of bounce and fun!

Why we love dogs

Dogs make wonderful pets and quickly become part of the family. A pet dog will make you laugh, be there for a hug when you feel sad, and enjoy playing games with you. In return, you must take good care of your pet.

First puppy

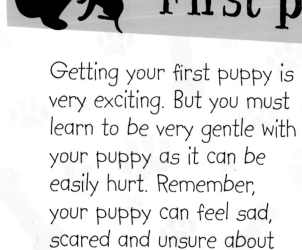

Getting your first puppy is very exciting. But you must learn to be very gentle with your puppy as it can be easily hurt. Remember, your puppy can feel sad, scared and unsure about things, just like you.

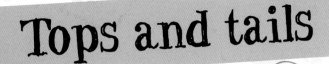

Tops and tails

Watching how your puppy uses its ears, head and tail will tell you a lot about how it is feeling. Learning about your puppy's **body language** will be very rewarding.

Best friends

Your puppy has a lot to learn and you will need to help it. Be gentle so that your puppy grows to trust you. You and your puppy will then become best friends, and your puppy will grow into a dog that loves you and wants to spend time with you.

What's your perfect pet?

Try this quick, fun quiz to see if a dog is the perfect pet for you. Write your answers – a, b or c – on a piece of paper.

 Is anybody home?
a) Someone is at home all day.
b) Someone is at home for most of the day.
c) The whole family is out all day.

 Time to play?
a) I will have lots of time to play with my pet.
b) I might have some time at weekends.
c) I'm quite busy with other things.

 Who loves walkies?
a) We'll take my pet on long walks every day.
b) Do we have to go if it's raining?
c) We can drive it around in the car.

 What will you do if you go on holiday?
a) We'll find a nice kennel for my pet to stay in.
b) We'll ask a neighbour to look after it.
c) That could be a problem.

5 Do you have a garden?

a) We've got a big garden.
b) We live opposite a park.
c) No, we don't have a garden.

6 Which of these things is most important for your dog to have?

a) Proper training.
b) Lots of love and care.
c) Toys to play with.

Count up how many 'a's, 'b's, and 'c's you wrote, and check out the results below.

Mainly 'a's
You'd be just right to own a dog! If you have lots of time to spend with your pet, and a big garden, you could choose a lively, medium-size dog, such as a spaniel, or a smaller **breed**, such as a Jack Russell. Both need plenty of walking, playing and proper training!

Mainly 'b's
Dogs need lots of exercise and someone to be at home with them for most of the day. It sounds like you have a busy life, so choose a pet that will be easier to look after and won't take up so much of your time. Don't choose a dog that needs lots of **grooming** and long walks.

Mainly 'c's
All dogs need exercise and someone to take care of them every day – so maybe a dog is not the right pet for you at the moment. Talk to your family or your local animal **rescue centre** about what sort of animal would make the best pet for you.

Choosing your puppy

There are many different breeds of dogs, so it's important to choose the one that is best for you and the way you live. Ask your vet or a rescue centre for advice, and check out the popular breeds on pages 42 to 59.

Needing a home

Choose me!

Rescue centres usually have a number of puppies needing good homes. The people who work there will be happy to help you choose the right puppy, and tell you how to look after it.

The right size

Remember – a small puppy can grow into a very big dog! Small dogs can be easier to handle than big dogs, but not all small dogs get on well with children. While all dogs need plenty of exercise, most large breeds will need more than smaller dogs.

Hairy or smooth?

Think about how much time you will have to look after your dog. A dog with long hair will need plenty of washing and brushing, and regular trips to the **grooming parlour**.

Your puppy's life cycle

A pregnant female dog will look for somewhere cosy and quiet to have her puppies. She will usually have a litter of between four and eight puppies, which she must feed and care for.

Just born

Puppies are born blind and deaf. They find their way to their mother's milk using their sense of smell. Newborn puppies sleep a lot and cuddle up to each other for warmth.

10 days old and so cute!

2 to 4 weeks old

When they are about two weeks old, puppies start to open their eyes. They can hear loud noises that may frighten them, and are just learning to walk.

4 to 8 weeks old

At four weeks old, puppies can eat solid food, walk, run, climb and play. They squeal and yelp as they jump about.

Leaving Mum

When puppies are between 8 and 12 weeks old, they are old enough to leave their mother and go to a new home.

Your puppy shopping list

Before you bring your puppy home, make sure you have everything that you need. Make a list and do a special doggy shop.

 Two bowls: one for food and one for water. Put these on newspaper, a mat or a tray on the floor, and make sure the room is quiet.

 A special spoon or fork for serving your puppy its food.

A dog bed – or put a soft blanket or an old, clean bath towel in a box. Put the bed somewhere warm and quiet.

A **pet carrier** for trips to the vet.

 A collar with your puppy's name and your address or phone number on it, and a lead.

 Rubber bones and other types of **chewy toy** to keep your puppy's teeth strong and healthy.

 A soft, cuddly toy. Buy one made especially for dogs.

 A **crate** for when your puppy travels in the car.

 Puppy food and special **treats**.

 A brush, comb or rough **mitt** for grooming your puppy.

Puppy's new home

The first few days in a new home can be a stressful time for a puppy. It will miss its mother, brothers and sisters, and it will have lots of new things to get used to.

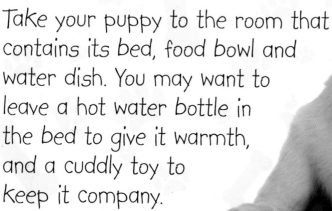

Settling in

Take your puppy to the room that contains its bed, food bowl and water dish. You may want to leave a hot water bottle in the bed to give it warmth, and a cuddly toy to keep it company.

20

Cosy crate

Introduce your puppy to its crate. Soon the puppy will happily go in and out of the crate and treat it as its special place.

Making friends

If you have other pets, leave your puppy in the crate for short periods and give them a chance to get used to the puppy's look and smell. It can take several weeks for animals to get used to each other, so don't leave them alone during this time.

Visit to the vet

You should take your puppy to the vet within the first two days of bringing it home. Ask about **vaccinations** that will help to keep your puppy safe from dangerous diseases.

Microchipped!

A vet can put a **microchip** under your puppy's skin – it's as small as a grain of rice, and has its own special number. The number is linked to a database that holds your address and phone number. If your puppy ever gets lost, a vet can use a special machine to read the microchip and quickly get in touch with you.

Fleas and worms

Ask your vet about **worming** your puppy. Regular worming is important because worms can make your pet ill. Your puppy should be wormed every two weeks. If your puppy is scratching a lot, it may have **fleas**. Ask the vet how to get rid of them.

Signs of illness

If you think your puppy is ill, take it to the vet. Look out for these signs that your puppy is not well: not eating or drinking, not playing, runny eyes and nose, runny poo, being sick, not breathing properly, limping, not going to the toilet properly.

23

Going out

Your puppy will love to play in the garden, but you need to keep it safe outside. Make sure there is no way your puppy can escape from the garden into the road.

Garden safe

When your puppy is in the garden, make sure someone watches it all the time. You need to make sure it won't get stuck under a gate or in a fence, or try to eat garden plants that may make it sick.

Staying at home

Your puppy should not go out on the street until it has had two lots of vaccinations – one at 8 weeks old, and one at 10 weeks. Vaccinations protect it against illnesses that it could pick up from other dogs.

On the street

Until your puppy is street-trained, always keep it on a lead when you take it for a walk. Keep your puppy close to you if you are near traffic, or if there are other animals nearby.

No sticks

Do not throw sticks for your puppy to chase. They could easily break into sharp splinters that could get stuck in your puppy's mouth or throat.

Handle with care

Puppies can easily get hurt, so always handle your puppy very gently. Don't walk around carrying your puppy, and never, ever drop it.

Proper pick-up

To pick up your puppy without hurting it, put one arm under its chest and the other arm under its bottom. Don't let its legs dangle down, and never pick it up by putting your arm around its middle.

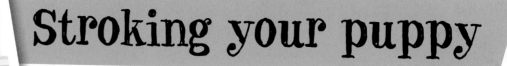
Stroking your puppy

Stroke your dog from its shoulders towards its tail. Don't pat it on the head – most dogs see this as a threat. Some puppies like to be gently scratched behind the ears. As you get to know your pet, you will soon learn what it likes and doesn't like.

Be gentle

Never hit your puppy, even if it is naughty. Shouting and hitting your pet will confuse it and make it scared of you. Never pull your puppy's ears or tail, or throw things at it – even in play.

Shhh!

If your puppy is asleep, don't wake it up. Puppies need a lot of sleep. Don't scare your pet by making loud noises near it.

27

Time for a brush

Grooming a puppy will help it get used to being brushed and combed, and will make the bond between you and your pet stronger. Grooming also helps to get rid of dirt and loose hair, and keeps your dog's skin in good condition.

Make mine a comb!

Make mine a mitt!

Brush or mitt?

Long-haired dogs will need to be groomed with a brush and a comb. A short-haired puppy will need a rough mitt. Ask for advice from a good pet shop, or speak to your vet.

Brush work

To groom your puppy, brush gently along its back and sides in the direction that its fur grows. Then, brush underneath its tummy and around its tail. Comb tangles very carefully so that you don't hurt your puppy.

Slicker brush for medium to long hair

Comb

Rough mitt

Rake brush for thick hair

Stress free

Your puppy might try to grab the comb or brush, thinking it's a game. Say no quietly but firmly, and keep on brushing. Your puppy may not like being brushed. Don't stress your pet – try grooming in short sessions, and reward your pet with a treat at the end of each session.

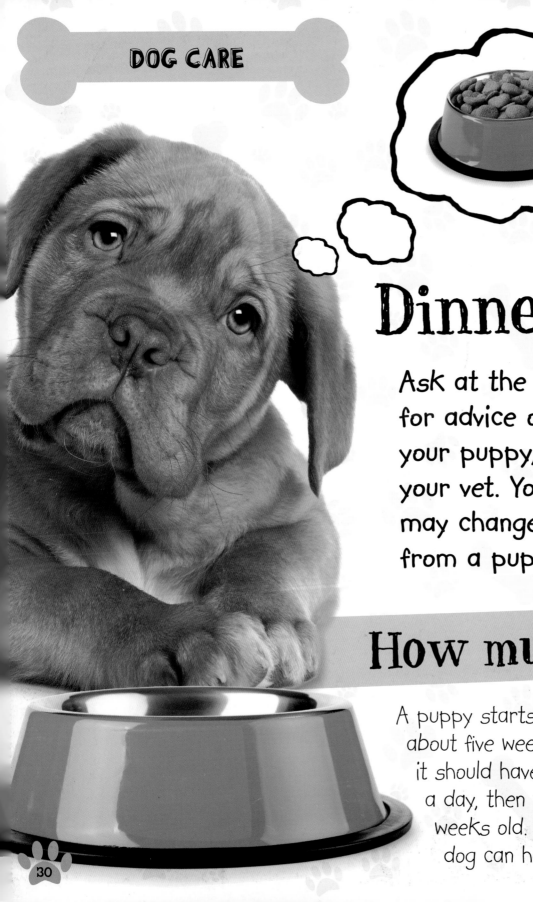

Dinner time!

Ask at the rescue centre for advice on what to feed your puppy, or speak to your vet. Your pet's diet may change as it grows from a puppy into a dog.

How much food?

A puppy starts to eat solid food at about five weeks old. To start with, it should have four small meals a day, then three when it is 12 weeks old. At six months your dog can have two meals a day.

Lots of water

Make sure your pet always has a bowl of clean water to drink, even during the winter months. Like humans, dogs need lots of water to stay healthy.

Tasty treats

Only give your puppy special puppy treats. Never feed your dog chocolate, as this can poison it. Do not give your pet sweets, biscuits, cake or too much human food. Dogs are greedy and will eat almost anything, but it's not good for them. Even foods such as grapes can be dangerous for some dogs.

Not eating

If your pet doesn't eat for more than a day, or gets sick after eating a couple of times, take it to the vet straight away for a check-up.

Playtime

Playing with your puppy is a great way to get to know each other. It's great fun too! Make sure the toys you choose are well made and safety tested. If your puppy chews bits off the toy, throw it away and buy a new one.

Old clothes

Don't give your puppy old clothes or shoes to play with. It won't know the difference between clothes that are toys and those that aren't, and will end up chewing your clothes too.

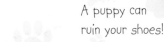

A puppy can ruin your shoes!

Chewy toys

Make sure the toys you buy are not too big for your puppy. Chewy rubber toys and balls are great for your puppy's teeth, but never throw toys or balls at your puppy, as they could hurt it.

Play bow

As your puppy gets older, he will tell you when he wants to play. A dog is asking to play when it puts his head low to the ground and his bottom and tail high in the air.

Grrrrrr!

Some puppies may growl when they are playing, and pretend to be fierce while mock fighting. Usually this is fine, but leave the toys and find an adult if your puppy starts to snarl and show its teeth.

Out and about

Your puppy needs exercise and fresh air to stay fit and healthy. Puppies should have no more than two 20-minute walks a day while their bones are still growing. After the age of one year, most dogs will love as much exercise as you can give them.

Walkies!

Taking your puppy for a walk every day is good exercise for both of you. While you are training your puppy, keep it on a lead until it learns its name and comes when it is called.

Great smells!

Some puppies will enjoy sniffing at everything. Give them time to have a good sniff at leaves and grass, but make sure they don't eat anything nasty.

Hello!

Saying hello!

Your puppy may want to say hello to all the other dogs. Be careful that bigger dogs don't scare your little puppy. Also be careful that your bouncy puppy doesn't jump all over other people or dogs. Most people won't mind, but some might!

"I like my hair long!"

Big or small? Choose a pet to suit you.

What a line-up – how many breeds can you name?

2
DOG BREEDS

Look at all the different types, or breeds, of dogs lined up at the bottom of this page. There are many, many more! Choose a breed to suit your home and the way you live.

Different breeds

A breed is a type of dog, such as a poodle or a beagle. There are lots of different breed groups – for example, **sporting**, **toy**, **terrier**, **working** or herding breeds. Some breeds do special jobs, such as rescuing people.

Farm dogs

Some dogs help farmers with their work. Border collies are great at rounding up sheep or **herding** them into pens. Old English sheepdogs are used for rounding up cattle, sheep and even reindeer.

Border collie

Old English sheepdog

Snow dogs

Husky dogs come from cold and snowy countries, such as Alaska, Siberia and Greenland. They have an extra-thick coat of fur to keep them warm. These dogs are trained to pull sleds across ice.

Lap dogs

Little dogs, such as this perky Yorkshire terrier, were bred to be small so that they could sit on a person's lap. They were kept as pets by rich people and royalty.

Breed needs

Spaniel

Different breeds of dogs need to be looked after in different ways. Some dogs, such as West Highland terriers, need to eat special food so they don't get skin problems. Spaniels are very active dogs, so they need lots of exercise and open space where they can race around and chase balls.

All shapes and sizes

Dogs come in many shapes and sizes. Their coats may be long or short, and come in a wide range of colours and patterns.

Miniature pinscher

Husky

Labrador retrievers

Coat colours

All dogs of the same breed look similar, but they can have different coloured coats. These lovely Labrador retrievers have black, chocolate and honey coats.

All sizes

Look at how different dogs can be. Some are so small they can fit in your hands. Others are almost as big as a small pony!

Big...

Most big dogs need lots of exercise, so you will need to find the time to take them out for long walks every day.

...and small

Small dogs are a good choice if you don't have a big house, but some small dogs don't like to be pulled about by very young children, and might growl or give them a nip.

Great Dane

Rottweiler

Miniature pinschers

Labrador retriever

Chihuahua

41

Afghan hound

The glamorous Afghan is one of the oldest dog breeds. Its long, silky coat is beautiful, but needs a lot of brushing.

Airedale

This terrier is sturdy and can be stubborn, but is easy to train.

Akita

The first akita dogs were bred in Japan. Now there is also an American akita, which is slightly bigger and heavier than the Japanese type.

American akita

American cocker spaniel

This breed is similar to the English cocker spaniel. It has a long coat and a sweet face, and is very easy to get along with.

Basset hound

The basset hound's long ears are called 'leathers'. This dog has a very long body, which means several children can pet it at once!

Beagle

Beagles are clever and make great family pets. They are affectionate, lively and always ready for action.

Bearded collie

These dogs were bred to work on farms. They have a long, shaggy and waterproof coat. Part of their coat hangs down from their chin and looks like a beard. They are lively and friendly, and need lots of exercise!

Bernese mountain dog

This breed was started in Switzerland for herding sheep and cattle. It was also used for pulling small carts. In the past it was called 'Gelbbacken', which means 'yellow cheeks'!

Bichon frisé

The story goes that sailors from hundreds of years ago found this breed on the island of Tenerife, off the coast of West Africa. The bichon frisé is a happy little dog that loves attention, but it also needs lots of grooming.

Border collie

These hardworking dogs are used for herding sheep. They are also used by **rescue services** to find people trapped under buildings that have collapsed in a hurricane or other disaster.

Borzoi

The name of this breed means 'swift' in its home country of Russia. It is also known as the Russian wolfhound. The beautiful borzoi is fast and graceful. It has a long, silky coat that gets easily tangled. Borzoi are quiet dogs that rarely bark.

Boxer

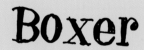

Many people say that once you have owned a boxer, you'll never want any other type of dog. It is energetic and fun-loving, and needs plenty of exercise.

Briard

This handsome dog has a flowing coat of black and different shades of brown. As well as its long fur, it has a beard, moustache and eyebrows that all need regular grooming. It is gentle, sweet-natured and loves to play.

Cavalier King Charles spaniel

This spaniel and the King Charles spaniel are happy dogs that love lots of exercise and being around people. They will not be happy if left alone at home all day.

Chihuahua

This is the smallest breed of dog in the world, but it doesn't know it! The cheeky Chihuahua has a big personality.

Chow

The chow comes from China, and was unknown to the rest of the world for a long time. Its tongue is bluey-black!

Dachshund

Miniature short-haired dachshund

The dachshund is a working dog from Germany. Although small, it needs lots of exercise. Its long spine can be easily damaged, so it needs to be handled carefully. It can also be hard to **house-train**. There are three types of dachshund: wire-haired, miniature long-haired and miniature short-haired.

Dalmatian

In the past, the Dalmatian ran alongside horse-drawn carriages and ahead of fire engines, so it became known as the 'firehouse dog'. It is a friendly breed. Dalmatian puppies are born white. Their spots only start to show as they get older.

Doberman pinscher

This clever dog is easy to train and will be a loyal and loving friend. Dobermans are strong dogs, so they need to be around people who can train and handle them properly.

German shepherd

The German shepherd was bred to herd cattle. It is hardworking, loyal and easy to train. It is often used by police for catching criminals, and by blind people as a **guide dog**. It needs lots of exercise and plenty of training.

Golden retriever

This breed is always happy. Golden retrievers love to play and enjoy being part of the family.

Great Dane

This is one of the biggest breeds of dog. These giants are very gentle and will be a loving family pet, but they need a big house and garden!

Havanese

These lively little dogs may be small, but they love a bit of rough and tumble! Remember always to be gentle with any dog.

Husky

The husky has a thick double coat that keeps it warm in the icy countries that it comes from. A husky's eyes can be brown or blue, or one of each! The husky is friendly, but needs lots of exercise.

Irish setter

These glamorous dogs have a beautiful, silky coat. They are good-tempered and love to be part of the family, but they do need long and regular walks.

Irish wolfhound

This mighty hound is the tallest of all dog breeds. Irish wolfhounds are friendly and loving, and make a great family pet, but they need a lot of space indoors because they are so big.

Jack Russell

There are two types of Jack Russell. The Parson Jack Russell has longer legs than the Jack Russell, but apart from that they look the same. These clever, energetic little dogs need to be well trained, otherwise they will get up to all sorts of mischief.

Labrador retriever

The Labrador retriever, or Labrador for short, is excellent with children and fun to be around. It needs long walks, and is always ready for a game or a swim. These dogs can easily become fat, so you must be careful not to overfeed them.

Lhasa apso

The Lhasa apso comes from Tibet, a country with high mountains and freezing cold weather. Its long fur has a thick undercoat, which helps to keep it warm. It also has hair over its eyes to protect them from wind, dust and bright sunshine.

Malamute

This big, strong dog was bred to pull heavy sleds in cold, snowy countries. It needs lots of exercise, and its fluffy coat should be brushed regularly.

Maltese

These little dogs were known as 'sleeve dogs' because they were carried around in a person's coat sleeve! Their dark eyes and nose stand out against their white coat.

Mastiff

These dogs might be big, strong and very heavy, but they are also gentle and loyal.

Newfoundland

A gentle giant, the huge Newfoundland is eager to please. As a puppy it looks like a cuddly teddy bear, but it quickly grows into a big, strong dog. These dogs love water and are superb swimmers.

Old English sheepdog

This dog has a long, shaggy coat that needs regular grooming. It should be taken on a daily walk or run so that it gets enough exercise. It is very protective.

Papillon

This tiny toy spaniel takes its name from the French word for butterfly, because of the shape of its wide, fringed ears. It is cute, intelligent and loves to make new friends.

Pekingese

In Ancient China, only the royal family were allowed to keep a Pekingese – ordinary city people were banned from owning them. Although it is small, the Pekingese is strong, brave, loving and playful.

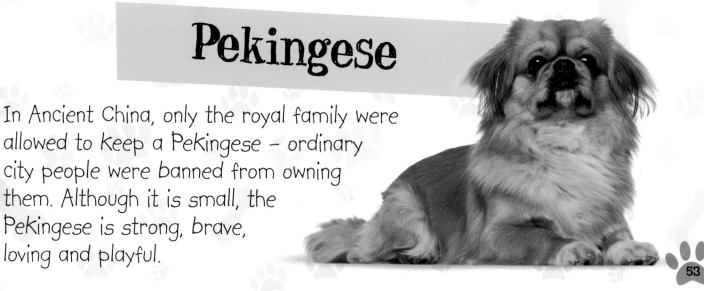

Pomeranian

This dainty little dog looks like a ball of fluff. It is clever and active, and needs lots of grooming and looking after.

Pug

The pug's little snub nose makes it snort and snore loudly! Pugs are smart, lively and love to be around people. They can easily get too hot, and must be kept cool when the weather is warm.

Puli

With its wild and woolly coat, it is sometimes difficult to see which way the puli is facing! It was originally used as a herding dog in Hungary, where its thick coat kept it warm.

Pyrenean mountain dog

Shepherds used this breed to guard their sheep from wolves, but it is a gentle and loving dog that makes an excellent pet. It is not very active and doesn't need much exercise, but it does need a lot of grooming.

Rottweiler

This big, strong dog can be a loving member of the family if it is trained properly. It needs lots of exercise and enjoys long walks.

Saluki

This slim dog can run very fast. It needs regular walks and runs to keep it fit and healthy. It might not get on with smaller pets, and needs lots of gentle, loving care.

Samoyed

The smiley Samoyed comes from Siberia – a cold and snowy part of Russia. It has a thick coat of fur to keep it warm in the freezing cold. These lively dogs need lots of exercise.

Schnauzer

The schnauzer was originally used to herd cattle and guard its owner's house and stables. It could also pull a small cart, making it an all-round farm dog.

Shar Pei

The Shar Pei was bred in China. Its skin has thick folds, and it always looks grumpy, but it is loving and loyal.

Shih tzu

This bundle of fluff has a long, flowing coat, big, dark eyes and a curved tail. The name 'shih tzu' comes from the Chinese word for lion. Shih tzus are bouncy and friendly, and make loyal and loving pets.

Scottish terrier

This dog is usually called a Scottie dog. Scotties are full of fun, friendly, playful and affectionate. They like to dig and need plenty of exercise and brushing.

Springer spaniel

Springer spaniels are gentle and loving, and can be working dogs, show dogs or great pets. They easily get excited, and will often spring or jump up into the air.

St Bernard

The St Bernard was originally bred as a rescue dog in the Swiss mountains. This big, strong dog is friendly, patient and clever.

Staffordshire bull terrier

The Staffordshire bull terrier, or Staffie, can have a bad reputation for being aggressive, but it loves to be around people and is good with children. It is gentle, fun-loving and playful, and makes a great family pet.

Poodle

Standard poodle

There are three sizes of poodle: standard, toy and miniature. Poodles love to be the centre of attention.

Vizsla

The vizsla is an energetic and loving pet. It is good-looking, intelligent and easy to train.

Welsh corgi

The corgi is the Queen of England's favourite dog, and she owns lots of them. Corgis are loyal, loving, intelligent and enjoy being with people.

West Highland terrier

This little dog is full of fun and has loads of energy. Its white coat needs regular brushing and trimming.

Yorkshire terrier

The tiny Yorkshire terrier is tougher than it looks. It loves to play. Its long, silky coat needs to be brushed every day to keep it soft and shiny.

A happy dog loves rolling over.

"I'm angry – stay away!"

"It's a great day for a run!"

3

HOW TO SPEAK DOG

From its nose to the tip of its waggy tail, your dog uses every bit of its body to talk to you. It will also make vocal sounds, such as barks and whimpers. Study your pet carefully and you'll soon be speaking dog too!

Understanding your dog

Dogs use their faces, ears and tails to tell us how they are feeling. Watch your pet closely and you will soon be able to understand what your pet is trying to say to you.

Feelings

Just like us, dogs have feelings. It is important to try and understand what your dog is feeling, so that you can give your friend the best life possible.

About you

Think about what you look and sound like from your dog's point of view. When you smile and show your teeth, you are being friendly, but to your dog this could mean trouble. When you play, you run, scream and shout. You're having fun, but your dog might think you are hurt or scared.

Talking together

Your dog is very clever. It will learn by your tone of voice when you are angry, being playful or asking it to do something. It will watch your face and your body language. Soon, you and your dog will understand each other perfectly!

Listen up!

Dogs make a range of sounds, such as **barks**, **woofs**, **yips**, **whines** and *growls*. Understanding your dog's sounds will allow you to 'read' how your dog is feeling.

Whines and whimpers

If a puppy makes a high-pitched whine, it may be feeling lonely or hungry. However, older dogs whine when they are excited, and instead whimper to express pain, fear or cold.

Hmmm...

Eeeep!

Yips

Yipping noises are produced when a dog makes a noise in its mouth while keeping its lips closed. Yips show a dog is feeling playful, or wants attention.

Howls

If a dog starts to howl, it could be trying to contact other members of its family. But if a dog howls during a song, it's probably just trying to sing along!

Ah-ooooh!

Woof! Woof!

Barks

Dogs bark for many reasons. This could mean they are bored, excited, looking for other dogs, or scaring off **intruders**.

Grrrr...

Growls

Just like humans, dogs can get upset or angry. A growling noise warns others to keep away.

A dog's nose knows

A dog's sense of smell is amazing. By sniffing, it learns important information about you, other dogs and the world around it.

Greeting a dog

Before you go near a dog, always ask its owner if the dog is good with children. If it is, hold out your fist for the dog to sniff. This helps the dog to get to know you. If the dog comes closer, it's saying it's happy to be touched.

Nosey!

From the moment it's born, a puppy has a great *sense of smell*. Even before it can see, hear or walk properly, it knows the smell of its mother, brothers and sisters, and it uses its sense of smell to find its mother's milk.

Who's been here?

When you go for a walk and your dog sniffs at walls, grass or a lamp post, it is picking up smells that have been left by other dogs. The smell is like a note, with information on who's been there and how long ago.

Sniff and learn

Dogs have lots of **glands** at the base of their tail that produce smells. When dogs meet, they sniff this area to find out as much as they can about the other dog.

Telling tails!

Your dog's tail can tell you a lot about how your dog is feeling. By watching its tail, you can see if your dog is happy, sad, scared or not sure about something.

Big wags

Dogs wag their tails a lot from side to side whenever they are excited or happy. Some dogs get so excited that their tails go round and round like a windmill! This is their way of giving people or other dogs a big grin!

Tail tucked under

If your dog tucks its tail under its body, lowers its head and puts its ears back a little, it may be feeling scared or unhappy. Dogs do this when they feel **threatened**. In the wild, dogs tuck their tail under to keep their soft tummy safe.

I'm scared.

I'm happy to see you!

Down or up?

When a dog comes towards you with its tail in the air, it usually means it is happy to see you. But if your dog is feeling a bit unsure about what is happening, it might keep its tail down and wag it slowly from side to side.

Body talk

A dog uses its whole body to let you know what it wants. Watch how it moves, sits and stands, and you'll soon be able to 'speak dog'.

Play with me!

Playtime

If your dog crouches down with its paws and front legs stretched out in front, its bottom up in the air and its tail wagging, it wants to play.

Jumping up

Your dog might jump and hop on its two back legs when it is very excited or pleased to see you. It might do this when you come home from shopping or from school. Your dog may also jump up when it is feeding time or time for a walk.

Welcome home!

Water, please!

Thirsty

Dogs pant when they are hot and thirsty. They will open their mouths slightly and breathe heavily. Some dogs let their tongues hang out. This helps them to cool down.

Keep away!

Growling

If your dog shows you its teeth or growls at you, keep away and do not touch it. It may be angry, hurt or scared, and there is a chance it could bite.

I see you...

Your dog will use its eyes to talk to you and to other dogs. When it looks longingly into your eyes, it may be asking for something, such as a walk or its dinner.

Don't stare

Do you feel uncomfortable when someone stares at you? Well, your dog feels the same way. For dogs, staring is rude, so they look away or to the side to be polite. Mother dogs stare at their puppies when they are naughty, so they soon learn that staring is bad news.

Blink and yawn

Some dogs blink a lot if they feel stressed, and they may give a big yawn. If your dog is yawning a lot, it might be feeling unhappy about something.

Dark eyes

If your dog is feeling down or unsure, its eyes might look more black than usual. This is because feeling afraid makes the dark centre of the eye – the pupil – get bigger. This happens to people when they are scared too.

Cheeky chops!

Dogs have a large mouth, a long tongue and big teeth. This is because in the wild they hunt prey and then eat it. Your dog's set of teeth is an amazing weapon.

Mega mouth!

Dogs use their mouths to eat, drink, pant, yawn, play and show how they feel. If your dog licks its lips or flicks its tongue over its nose, it might be feeling scared or stressed.

Eeek...

74

Types of teeth

The long fangs near the front of a dog's mouth are called **canine teeth**. Dogs use them for stabbing and tearing food. The teeth at the back of the mouth are called **molars**. These are good for chewing and crushing bones.

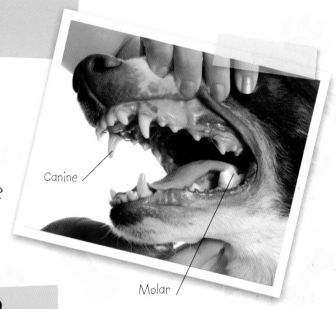

Canine

Molar

Look, no teeth!

When dogs show their teeth in a snarl, they are usually warning you to stay away. Dogs that are friendly and happy won't show their teeth. People do the opposite – we like to show our teeth when we're happy by giving a big smile!

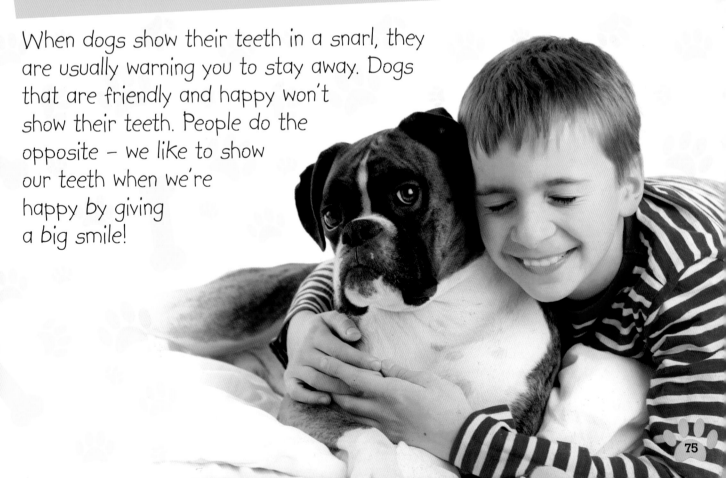

All ears!

When you are learning what your dog is feeling, you need to look at its mouth, head and ears. Most dogs use all three to let us know what they are feeling.

Ear, ear

Different breeds of dog have different types of ears. Some have long, floppy ears, some have upright ears that bend over at the top, and others have ears that stick straight up.

I'm ready!

The messages that small, upright ears send us are easy to see. For example, ears pointed upright and forwards show that a dog is alert and ready for action. Your dog will have these ears when it is time for a walk.

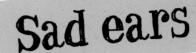

Sad ears

Ears that are held back or close to the head show that a dog is feeling scared or miserable about something. If its tail is also tucked under its body, it's probably feeling very unhappy.

I'm happy!

It's easy to tell when your dog is happy. A happy dog has bright eyes, a wagging tail and a friendly face that shows it is pleased to be part of the family.

Welcome home!

Your dog will be pleased to see you when you get home. If your dog jumps up to greet you, it is trying to get close to your face so that it can give you a welcome sniff or lick.

Love me

Most dogs love to be stroked. They ask for this by putting their head against you and looking up with soft eyes. Gently stroke your dog from its head down.

78

Hey – it's me!

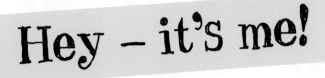

Your dog might touch you with its paw
if it wants attention. Dogs learn how
to do this when they are puppies –
they press their mum's belly with
their paws to ask for milk.

Shhh, dog snoozing...

Happy dogs love to play and sleep! Your
sleeping dog may sigh deeply, wag its tail
and make little sleepy noises. Some
dogs might snore loudly! Don't
touch your dog when it is
sleeping as this could scare
it and make it jump.

Beware of the dog

Just like people, dogs can become angry if they feel threatened or want to keep food or toys all to themselves! Most dogs would rather run away when they're scared, but if they can't, they may decide to attack.

Keep away

Grrrrr!

An angry dog will crouch down, growl and show its teeth and the whites of its eyes. If your dog does this, leave it alone and call an adult.

Ready to fight

If an angry dog wants to fight, it will stand with its ears pricked up and its head held high. The dog will stare and make the fur along its back (its hackles) stand up, which makes it look bigger.
Never go near a dog that looks like this, as it may try to bite.

Aawww...

Scared or hurt

A frightened dog will **cower** with its ears flattened, and it may bare its teeth. It might whine and whimper if it is in pain. If your dog is doing this, try and think why it could be scared. Has there been a loud noise, or has it hurt itself on something?

Panicky pup

Dogs show that they are unhappy by trying to hide or by getting ready to run away. If you spot these signs in a young dog, you can try to help it feel more confident – a bit like being its big brother or sister!

Disappearing act

Dogs often try to shrink when they feel threatened. They cower so that their body is low on the ground and tuck their paws underneath their body. They may also make their ears go flat and have wide, staring eyes.

Barking

When a dog barks, it is usually a sign that it is feeling some type of stress. Different barks mean different things – the dog may be lonely, bored or warning you that there's an intruder.

Keep calm

The best way to help your dog if it gets scared is to give it lots of space. Let your pet go to the place where it feels safest so that it can calm down. When your dog is feeling better and comes out of its safe place to see you again, make sure you give it plenty of **praise**.

Super senses

All dogs are very special. They have amazing senses of smell and sight, and can pick up signals that are invisible to humans.

I'm watching

Dogs watch everything that goes on around them. Some dogs even seem to know when we're going out or when visitors are about to arrive! This is because a dog can pick up tiny changes in the way we behave and the things we do. These changes tell the dog that something is about to happen.

Shoes on... walkies!

Dogs love to watch their owners for clues about what they are planning to do next. For example, when you put on your shoes, your dog will know you are about to go out for a walk, so it will start to get very excited!

Helper dogs

Because dogs have special senses, they can help us in lots of ways. Guide dogs help blind people to lead safe and normal lives and hearing dogs help deaf people. Some dogs help to look after people in wheelchairs. Other dogs, called **sniffer dogs**, find people trapped in collapsed buildings.

Guide dogs wear a special harness.

Sniffer dogs in Turkey help search for earthquake victims.

85

Training creates a bond between you and your dog.

"This is fun! Just watch me go!"

Reward your dog for doing well.

4

TRAINING AND TRICKS

It is important to train your dog to behave both inside and outdoors. It's also fun to learn tricks together. Training needs a lot of patience, but it is very rewarding and will create a special bond between you and your pet.

Why train your puppy?

It's funny to watch your puppy getting into mischief once in a while, but a puppy that isn't trained can cause a lot of damage around the house.

Oh no!

Take shoes away from your puppy and firmly say "no!"

Puppies love to chew, pull and tug. They are just playing, but it won't be fun if you've got to clear up the mess or buy a new pair of shoes.

Not so little

Naughty puppies can *be* cute, but soon your puppy will *become* an adult dog, which you won't want misbehaving. You need to train dogs when they are little so that they get into good habits for when they are older.

Teach your dog not to pull while it's still young.

Free to run

A well trained dog is much safer to take out for walks and will be much easier to handle when meeting new people or other dogs. If your dog is well trained, you can let it off its lead to run around and play.

All grown up

Training a puppy can take time. If you don't have much time as a family, why not think about adopting a fully grown dog that has already been trained? Speak to your local rescue centre about it – there are hundreds of lovely dogs out there looking for their forever home.

Rewards

Starting to train your puppy is easy. You just need a little space and some quiet time so you and your puppy can both concentrate. Make sure you have lots of tasty treats at the ready, and make it fun!

Great treats

The best way to train a puppy or dog is to reward it with lots of praise and treats when it does as it's told. If it doesn't do as it's told, no reward should be given until it does. Never, ever hit or shout at your puppy or dog as this will make it afraid of you and could hurt it.

Short and sweet

Keep training sessions between 5 and 15 minutes long because a puppy can lose concentration easily. It's usually best to train your puppy when it's hungry, as this will make it more eager to earn a reward.

What is a reward?

When you are training your dog or puppy, you need to be able to give it lots of small rewards in a short space of time. This means plenty of food treats. Some puppies and dogs love shop-bought treats. Others enjoy pieces of fruit or vegetables. Always check with an adult that the type and amount of food you're using is right for your dog or puppy.

Apple

Dog biscuits

Carrot

House rules

It's important that your puppy gets into a routine in its new home. This will help it to feel happy and secure. Agree on some **house rules** for your puppy with the rest of the family, and make sure that you all follow them.

Sleep well

Decide on where your puppy is going to sleep, and stick to it. If you let your puppy sleep under your duvet when its small and cute, it'll want to do the same when it's large and muddy!

Table manners

Never feed your dog from the table or from your plate while you are eating. Ask your dog to go to its bed – even if you are only eating a snack. Give it a chewy toy to keep it happy.

Dog words

sit
lie down
stay here
leave it

To help your dog understand what you want, everyone in the family must use the same words of **command**. For example, if you want your dog to lie down, decide whether you want to say "down" or "lie down". Once you have decided which words you are going to use, make a list and stick it on the fridge door for everyone to see!

Toilet matters!

Dogs are very clean and, if possible, will always choose to go to the toilet away from where they sleep. However, you still need to teach your pet to be clean around the house.

Gently does it

When you bring your puppy home, take it outside so that it can go to the toilet if it needs to, and get to know where its toilet is. Don't let it go beyond the garden until it has had all of its vaccinations.

Lots of praise

To help your puppy go to the toilet in the right place, take it outside every time it wakes up, after playtime and after eating and drinking. Give it lots of praise when it goes. A three-month-old puppy will usually need to go to the toilet every three hours.

Don't shout

Dogs and puppies should never be shouted at if they accidentally go to the toilet indoors. This will only make them more nervous. Simply say "no!" firmly, and then move them to their outdoor spot.

Getting started

As soon as you meet your new puppy, start using its name. Over time, it will get to know your voice and recognize its name. You can then teach it to come to you when you call.

What's my name?

Practise this exercise anywhere and everywhere.

1 Stand in front of your dog. Say your dog's name in a happy voice.

2 As soon as your pet looks at you, say "good" and give it a treat. Saying this will tell your pet that it's done well.

3 Repeat this three or four times.

"Here, Patch!"

Before you let your dog off its lead outside, you must make sure it will come to you when it is called.

1 Start your training indoors. Stand a few steps away from your dog and call it using a friendly voice. For example, you could say "here, Patch!" or "come".

2 Show your pet a treat to encourage it to come to you. Even if your dog only moves one step towards you, say "good" and then give it the treat by dropping it on the floor in front of you.

3 Increase the distance your dog has to come to get the treats, making sure you give it plenty of praise. If your dog likes to play with toys, you could play a game with it as a reward too.

4 Practise calling your dog while you are in the house and do the same when you are in the garden. Always give your pet a treat when it comes to you.

New people and places

It is important that your puppy gets to meet new people and visit lots of different places. This will help it to grow up confident and happy.

Correct collar

Before your puppy or dog can experience new things, you'll have to train it to walk on a lead without pulling or tugging. But first, make sure its collar is not done up too tight – an adult should be able to slip two fingers under it.

Lead on...

Let your puppy get used to having a lead on. Clip the lead to the collar and leave your puppy to walk around the house for short periods of time. Then you can start training.

Walking to heel

1 Start with your dog in the sit position on your left side. Keep its lead quite short so the dog stays close to your body. Hold the other end of the lead in your right hand, and a food treat in your left hand.

2 Start walking. Say your dog's name, and then say "heel", keeping your dog close to your left side.

3 When your dog keeps to heel for a few steps, give it a small treat. Soon your dog will stop trying to pull away.

"Sit" and "shake paws"

If your dog is sitting, it can't run away, jump up, chase things, steal shoes or chew toys!

"Sit"

1 Call your dog towards you by saying "here", and show it the food treat.

2 Move your hand with the treat over your dog's head. It will try to keep its eyes on the food, and should start to sit. Don't hold the treat too high or your dog will jump up to get it.

3 As your dog starts to sit, say "sit" and then give it the treat. Once your dog has learnt the "sit" command, you can start training it to sit when you're facing it from the side, the front or from behind.

"Shake paws"

This is a cute trick that makes it look as though your dog is shaking hands!

1 Command your dog to sit in front of you. Give it a treat.

2 Hold another treat tightly in your hand, which should be close to the floor. Now, watch your dog carefully! Say "good" and release the treat as soon as your dog moves its paw. Most dogs will initially attempt to sniff at the food with their nose or mouth. If you hold on to the food, your dog will try to get the treat by touching your hand with its paw. Give it the treat. Repeat at least four times.

3 Move the hand that is holding the treat upwards, saying "good" as you do so. Your dog will have to reach up higher to touch you with its paw. Praise your pet and give it the treat.

4 Carry on practising, but instead of saying "good", say "shake paws" or "paw". Soon enough your clever pet will shake hands on command.

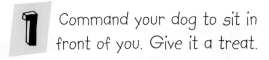

"Lie down" and "stay"

As your puppy gets older, you can teach it more difficult commands. "Stay" is useful if you need your dog to stop suddenly to keep it safe from danger.

"Lie down"

1 Hold a food treat close to your dog's nose. Then slip the treat under your thumb so your dog knows it is still there but can't see it!

2 Lower your hand slowly to the floor until it is between your dog's front paws. Keep the treat firmly in the palm of your hand, under your thumb.

3 Your dog will try to burrow its nose under your hand to lick the treat. You will see its front end go down, or it will move backwards slightly. Be patient – your pet will eventually flop to the floor.

Now "stay"

Teach your dog to stay in the sitting or lying down position. This is an important command for your dog to learn as you can use it to keep your pet safe when you are out together.

1 Ask your dog to sit or lie down by saying "stay". Count to two, then say "good" and give the treat.

2 Ask your dog to sit or lie down by saying "stay". Wait five seconds, then say "good" and give the treat.

3 Repeat, but this time wait for seven seconds, then say "good" and give the treat.

4 Ask your dog to sit or lie down, saying "stay". Count to 30, then say "good" and give lots of treats! Now, whenever you say "stay" your dog should lie down and only move when you say "good". Repeat at least four times.

4 When your dog lies down, say "good" and release the treat from your hand so your dog can eat it.

5 Repeat this several times – sometimes with the food in your hand and sometimes without. When your dog lies down after following your hand to the floor, say the words "lie down" just before you move your hand.

"Fetch!"

Dog rope

Some dogs, such as Labradors, love to fetch items, while others need training. You can play fetch using a special dog ball, frisbee or dog rope.

Bring it back

1 Hold the object in your hand and offer it to your dog. If your dog sniffs it, say "good" and then give it a treat. Repeat this a few times.

2 Next you want your dog to take the object in its mouth. If it does, let your dog hold it for a second, then say "good" and give a treat. Build up the time your pet holds the object to about 20 seconds.

3 Now put the object on the floor. You can wiggle it and make it move like a snake, but don't throw it.

4 As soon as your dog grabs hold of the toy, let the toy go and move backwards. Encourage your dog to come to you and then ask it to give you the toy.

5 Now train your dog to fetch outdoors. Just before you throw the ball, say "fetch". When your dog brings the toy back and drops it, give it praise and a treat. As your dog gets to know the word "fetch", increase the distance that you throw the toy.

Spin trick

Some dogs can be taught to spin around on a doormat, so they wipe their paws when they come in!

Wipe your feet!

1 Hold a food treat in one hand. Move your hand around in a big, wide circle to make your dog follow. Do this until your dog's head nearly meets its tail. As soon as it has gone full circle, say "good" and give a tasty treat.

2 Repeat this several times until your dog starts to follow your hand each time you move it around in a circle.

106

3 Now move your hand without a treat in it so that your dog starts to turn around when it sees your hand signal. Say "good", give lots of praise and offer a reward if your pet spins the whole way round.

4 It's time to add the command! Say "spin" just before you start to move your hand. Practise this many times until your dog begins to move each time you say the word "spin".

Hands free!

To make this trick look really good, it's best if your dog spins to a word rather than a hand signal. Stand upright and ask your dog to "spin". If it does, say "good" and give a whole handful of treats! Your pet is a genius, after all! If your dog hesitates or looks confused, make a tiny movement with your hand to help it figure things out!

Figure of eight

Teaching your dog to move in a figure of eight around your legs requires skill. Take your time. Teach this trick slowly and carefully, especially if you have short legs or a big dog!

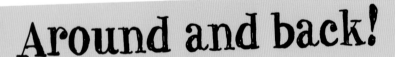

Around and back!

1 Stand still, holding a food treat in each hand. Make sure you have space around you so that you don't fall on anything dangerous if you do get tangled up.

2 Starting with your dog on your left, bend your right knee forwards and lure your dog under your right leg while holding the treat in your right hand.

3 Say "good" and give the dog a treat.

4 Repeat this several times until your dog is really confident at passing under your bent leg.

5 Now repeat again, but instead of giving the treat after your dog has passed under your right leg, immediately show that you have a treat in your left hand too, behind your left knee. Lure your dog under your left leg, then say "good" and give the treat.

6 Put the two movements together. You will find that your dog is doing a figure of eight through your legs! Practise this a number of times and give lots of treats and praise. Ignore your dog if it makes a mistake – just try again instead!

7 After a while, practise the trick without holding food in your hands. Then, start to prompt your dog by moving your knee rather than luring with your hands. Quick dogs can even weave in and out of your legs while you are walking along! Always be careful not to tread on your dog's toes.

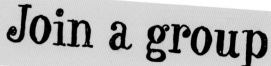

Dog sports

Having fun with your dog is a great way to make new friends and learn new skills. It will also keep your dog fit and lively.

Join a group

See if there is a local dog **agility club** for your family to join. Your dog will learn to jump hurdles, run through tunnels and walk along high beams – a bit like showjumping for dogs. Any breed can have a go, but your dog must be more than one year old to take part in jumping.

Fun run!

If you have a big enough garden, you could get the family together to make a mini obstacle course for your dog.

1 Make a mini seesaw for your dog by balancing a plank of wood on a log stump.

3 Attach a play tunnel to the ground. These are available from most good toy stores and make a great present for you or your dog.

2 Hold a hoop upright on the ground and encourage your dog to walk through it by offering a treat. When your dog is happy doing this, raise the hoop slightly so the dog has to jump through!

Watch out!

Make sure there are no sharp or glass objects lying around, and move items that might splinter or snap and hurt you or your dog. Has everything been set up safely? Then get ready... steady... go!

Glossary

agility club A special club where you can go to train your dog by taking it over an obstacle course. The dog learns to zig-zag between poles, jump over hurdles and run through tunnels.

breed A group of dogs that shares certain features, such as size and shape, and sometimes coat colour. Some breeds are trained to do certain jobs, such as herding.

body language The way a dog uses its body, tail and face to tell you what it wants.

canine teeth The four long, pointed teeth near the front of a dog's mouth. Dogs use these teeth to rip and tear meat.

chewy toy A special dog toy usually made of rubber that dogs can chew without harming their teeth.

command A word that your dog must learn to obey, such as "sit".

cower When a dog tries to make itself smaller by crouching down low and holding its ears and tail close to its body. Dogs do this when they are frightened.

crate A special cage where your dog can feel safe. The crate should be big enough to allow your dog to stand up, stretch and turn around.

fleas Small insects that may live on your dog and make it scratch. Fleas can make a dog sore and ill if you don't get rid of them.

glands Parts of the body that you can't see, but that give off certain smells.

grooming When you brush and comb your dog.

grooming parlour A place where you can take a dog to have its coat washed, brushed and trimmed, and its nails cut.

guide dog A dog that has been specially trained to help blind people do everyday tasks, such as crossing roads safely.

herding Keeping together a group of animals, such as cattle or sheep, and making sure they move in a certain direction.

house rules The rules that a family sets for its dog – for example, not allowing it to be fed from the table, or letting it sleep on people's beds.

house-train Making sure your puppy behaves well at home and doesn't go to the toilet in the house.

intruders Unwelcome strangers who come too close to a house. Many dogs bark to warn their family if strangers are approaching.

microchip A tiny piece of electronic equipment that a vet puts under the skin of a dog. Each microchip has its own special number, and this makes it possible for any vet to trace the owner of a lost dog.

mitt A brush that you can wear on your hand to groom a dog.

molars The large, flat-topped teeth at the back of a dog's mouth that the dog uses to chew food.

pet carrier A special box with a door, used for carrying puppies when they are very little – for example, to the vet.

praise Saying nice things to a dog when it has been good, such as "well done" and "good dog".

rescue centre
A place that looks after animals, such as dogs and puppies, when their owners no longer want them. The rescue centre will try to find them new forever homes.

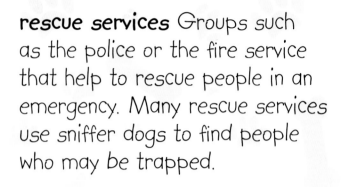

rescue services Groups such as the police or the fire service that help to rescue people in an emergency. Many rescue services use sniffer dogs to find people who may be trapped.

sniffer dogs Dogs that have been specially trained to sniff out either drugs and guns, or people trapped in damaged buildings or deep snow.

sporting dogs Dogs used by hunters to bring back, or retrieve, ducks, birds and other small wild animals that the hunters have shot.

terriers Dogs used for hunting and chasing. They are usually strong, active dogs that love to sniff and dig in the earth.

threatened The feeling that a dog has when it thinks a person or another dog is going to attack it.

toy dogs Small, often pretty, dogs, kept just as pets – for example, the Cavalier King Charles spaniel.

vet An animal doctor. You should take your dog to a vet if it is not well, has had an accident, or needs to be microchipped or vaccinated.

working dogs This group can include the herding dogs, but also dogs used as rescue dogs, guide dogs and sniffer dogs. Working dog breeds include St Bernards, doberman pinschers and huskies.

worming Giving a dog a special medicine that stops it from getting worms in its tummy, or that gets rid of the worms if the dog has already got them. Worming should be done regularly to keep a dog fit and healthy.

treats Dog biscuits or other small snacks that a dog really loves, such as little bits of sausage or cheese. Treats should be given as a reward when a dog has been good. You can also buy special treats for puppies from a vet or pet shop.

vaccinations Injections given by a vet that will help to stop a dog becoming ill or catching diseases from other dogs.

Index

Notes for parents and teachers

Owning a dog can be a wonderful experience for the whole family. However, it is also a big responsibility. Although this book has described certain dog care tasks that children can be involved in, the adults in the family are entirely responsible for the dog's wellbeing and the safety of children around it.

You should be certain that you can afford all necessary veterinary, training and kennel bills before getting a dog.

There should also be an adult at home most of the time, as it is unfair to leave a dog on its own for more than three hours a day.

Dog ownership can benefit children greatly as it can teach them about loyalty, responsibility and care. However, there are safety rules that you need to bear in mind to make dog ownership as enjoyable an experience as possible.

Safety check

Dogs need to be walked twice a day. The adults in the family should take responsibility for this, as it can be dangerous for a child under the age of 16 to keep control of a dog.

By law, you must take responsibility for cleaning up your dog's mess when you take it out for walks. Dog faeces can spread disease.

To protect young children from being knocked over or bitten, they should not be left alone with a dog, and only adult members of the family should feed the dog.

Do not allow a child to carry food near a dog, as the dog may try to snatch the food and knock the child over.

Children should be taught to stroke their dog – and any other dog – from the side and not from the front, and they should never pat its head. Head-patting is a dominant gesture that can make some dogs snap.

Parents' checklist

You, not your child, are responsible for the care of a puppy.

Please consider the following before you commit yourself to buying a puppy, as dogs can be very expensive:

- dog licence
- vet bills (*seek advice from your local vet*)
- food bills
- Kennel or dogsitting bills if you can't take your dog with you when you go away
- possible training fees – some puppies may need to attend obedience classes
- If you are out of the house for more than 3 to 4 hours a day, a dog is not a suitable pet for you.
- Do not keep even a small dog in cramped conditions.

- Are you willing to walk a dog twice a day? Your local area might also have 'pooper scooper' laws, so you must be prepared to clean up after your dog every day.
- Do you have any other pets? Will they get along with a dog?
- Always supervise pets and children.
- If you want to buy a purebred dog, do some research first.
- All dogs need vaccinations, worming and flea treatments. Spaying or neutering is recommended for all dogs. Ask your vet or local Humane Society for advice.

Picture credits

(t=top, b=bottom, l=left, r=right, c=centre, fc=front cover, bc=back cover)

Alamy
27cr © Tetra Images, 71tr © Janine Wiedel Photolibrary, 94tl © Frank Naylor, 111tc © Petra Wegner, 111cr © Juniors Bildarchiv GmbH, 111bl © Kuttig - People

Jane Burton
64tl

FLPA
fc (main) ImageBroker, bc cl ImageBroker, bc c Jeanette Hutfluss/Tierfotoagentur, bc cr Mark Raycroft/Minden Pictures, bc bl (left) Chris Brignell, bc bl (right) Chris Brignell, 2c Sigrid Starick/Tierfotoagentur, 13tr Imagebroker, 20tr Erica Olsen, 20tl Imagebroker, 21tr Imagebroker, Peter Faber/Imagebroker, 28bl Jeanette Hutfluss/ Tierfotoagentur, 38br Wayne Hutchinson, 39tl Ramona Richter/Tierfotoagentur, 39cr Ramona Richter/Tierfotoagentur, 40bl Dana Geithner/Tierfotoagentur, 42bl Chris Brignell, 42br Chris Brignell, 43tr Mark Raycroft/Minden Pictures, 43cl Chris Brignell, 43br Chris Brignell, 44tl Bernd Brinkmann/Imagebroker, 44cr Imagebroker, 44bl Chris Brignell, 45tr Yvonne Janetzek/Tierfotoagentur, 45cl Sigrid Starick, 46tr ImageBroker/Imagebroker, 46cl Arco Images, Wegner, Petra/Imagebroker, 46br Chris Brignell, 47tr Mark Raycroft/Minden Pictures, 48tr Chris Brignell, 48cl Stefan Ott/Tierfotoagentur, 48bl Ivonne Felgenhauer/Tierfotoagentur, 49cl Sigrid Starick/ Tierfotoagentur, 49br Mark Raycroft/Minden Pictures, 50tr Ivonne Felgenhauer/Tierfotoagentur, 50cl Simone Kochanek/Tierfotoagentur, 51tr Ivonne Felgenhauer/ Tierfotoagentur, 51br Sigrid Starick/Tierfotoagentur, 52tr ImageBroker/Imagebroker, 52cl Ivonne Felgenhauer/Tierfotoagentur, 53cl Sigrid Starick/Tierfotoagentur, 54tr Michaela Kuhn/Tierfotoagentur, 54cl Ramona Richter/Tierfotoagentur, 54br Heidi & Hans-Juergen Koch/Minden Pictures, 55tr Mark Raycroft/Minden Pictures, 55cl Ivonne Felgenhauer/Tierfotoagentur, 56tr Chris Brignell, 56cl Ramona Richter/Tierfotoagentur, 56br Chris Brignell, 57tr Sigrid Starick/Tierfotoagentur, 57cl Tierfotoagentur, 57br Chris Brignell, 58tr Imagebroker, Silke Klewitz-Seeman/Imagebroker, 58cl Chris Brignell, 58bl Ramona Richter/Tierfotoagentur, 59tr Ivonne Felgenhauer/Tierfotoagentur, 59cl Chris Brignell, 59bl Ingo Schulz/Imagebroker, 64cl ImageBroker/Imagebroker, 65tr Mark Raycroft/Minden Pictures, 65cl Chris Brignell, 65br Sigrid Starick, 67bl Ramona Richter/Tierfotoagentur, 84tr Chris Brignell

Getty Images
25cr LWA, 63br Purestock

Shutterstock
fc (collar) Nikolai Tsvetkov, fc (tag) tkemot, bc (background) Kateryna A., 1t tkemot, 1b Erik Lam, 2t Andresr, 2b Martin Valigursky, 2-3 Erik Lam, 3t tkemot, 4 Eric Isselee, 5t Robynrg, 5b Christian Mueller, 6-7 Erik Lam, 7tl Rita Kochmarjova, 8t Ilike, 8c Africa Studio, 8b fotoedu, 9l Francesco83, 9r Viorel Sima, 10tl Andresr, 10cl Dreamy Girl, 10br holbox, 11tl Eric Isselee, 11tr Fly_dragonfly, 11br Golden Pixels LLC, 12c oliveromg, 13bl Eric Isselee, 13bc Igor Kovalchuk, 13br fivespots, 14tl Erik Lam, 14tr Michiel de Wit, 14bl Roman Samokhin, 14-15 Eric Isselee, 15bc Eric Isselee, 16tl Brberrys, 16br Nixx Photography, 17tr Hannamariah, 17cl anquiam, 17br gurinaleksandr, 18 top to bottom: a) Nikolai Tsvetkov, b) taviphoto, c) Vitaly Korovin, d) Nikolai Tsvetkov, 19 top to bottom: a) violetblue, b) karen roach, c) Viktoria Gavrilina, d) Michael Pettigrew, e) WilleeCole Photography, f) Africa Studio, g) Ekaterina Kamenetsky, 20br Eric Isselee, 21cr Okeanas, 21br Okeanas, 22tl Ilike, 22br WilleeCole Photography, 23tr Ermolaev Alexander, 23bl Ilike, 24tl Javier Brosch, 24tr lantapix, 24br Distinctive Images, 24-25 Robert Adrian Hillman, 25tl VP Photo Studio, 26l MaszaS, 27tl Gina Smith, 27bl Jagodka, 28tr Scorpp, 29 left to right: a) Ekaterina Kamenetsky, b) Budimir Jevtic, c) Photofollies, d) Budimir Jevtic, e) cynoclub, 29bl cynoclub, 30cl Eric Isselee, 30bl Elnur, 30tr Elnur and Sergey Lavrentev, 31tr Yuriy Chertok, 31cl Photosebia, 31b Francesco83, 32tl Eric Isselee, 32br Eric

Isselee, 33tr Mila Atkovska, 33cl Julia Remezova, 33br danilobiancalana, 34cl Martin Valigursky, 34tr Michele Paccione, 34br Dmitry Naumov, 35tl cofkocof, 35tr Erik Lam, 35cl Michele Paccione, 35bl Utekhina Anna, 36tr PaulShlykov, 36cl pixshots, 36-37 Erik Lam, 38tr cynoclub, 38cl Erik Lam, 38bc Eric Isselee, 39bl Ermolaev Alexander, 40c Vivienstock, 41 Erik Lam, 42tr Raywoo, 45br Dora Zett, 47cl Nikolai Tsvetkov, 47br MindStorm, 49tr Eric Isselee, 50br Fly_dragonfly, 51cl Eric Isselee, 52br Eric Isselee, 53tr Eric Isselee, 53br Eric Isselee, 55br Anna Tyurina, 59cr Dan Kosmayer, 60t otsphoto, 60c Pshenina_m, 60b Lobke Peers, 60-61 WilleeCole Photography, 61c WilleeCole Photography, 62bl Javier Brosch, 62-63 Paul Cotney, 63tr AVAVA, 64br Eric Isselee, 66tl Dmitrij Skorobogatov, 66tr chaoss, 66bl Luis Carlos Torres, 67tr Tom Prokop, 67cr LarsTuchel, 68tl Mac-leod, 68br Eric Isselee, 69tr Vivienstock, 69bl Charlie Bard, 70tr phasinphoto, 70bl cynoclub, 71cl RazoomGame, 71br Viorel Sima, 72tl vvvita, 72br aleksandr hunta, 73tr Nikita Starichenko, 73br Anna Hoychuk, 74tr Sue McDonald, 74bl Aaron Amat, 75tr cynoclub, 75br Anna Hoychuk, 76tr Annette Shaff, 76bl Mat Hayward, 77tr Eric Isselee, 77bl Jagodka, 78tr sonya etchison, 78cl Andresr, 78br gurinaleksandr, 79tr Tom Wang, 79cr Susan Schmitz, 79b WilleeCole Photography, 80tl Tribalium, 80b cynoclub, 81tl cynoclub, 81br dogboxstudio, 82tl sakhorn, 82bl Erik Lam, 83tr Eric Isselee, 83b Annette Shaff, 84bl C_Gara, 85tr Javier Brosch, 85bl s_bukley, 85br fotostory, 86t sonya etchison, 86c Margo Harrison, 86b sonya etchison, 87l Andrey Eremin, 87r Marina Jay, 88tl holbox, 88tr weter.777, 89tr sianc, 89cl Christian Mueller, 89br Annette Shaff, 90tl Mandy Godbehear, 90tr Sasimoto, 90br Mandy Godbehear, 91b foods, left to right: a) Robyn Mackenzie, b) Africa Studio, c) jeehyun, 92tl (back) wrangler, 92tl (clock) Alex Staroseltsev, 92tl (bowl) Sbolotova, 92tr Sasimoto, 92br BaLL LunLa, 93tl mykeyruna, 93cr Roberaten, 93br Danny E Hooks, 94tr Sasimoto, 94br Joy Brown, 95tr Petr Jilek, 95bl Gelpi JM, 95bc Susan Schmitz, 96tl Vietrov Dmytro, 97tr Mat Hayward, 98tl Julie Campbell, 98tr Accent, 99tr weter 777, 100tr Golden Pixels LLC, 100cl Sasimoto, 102tr majivecka, 104tr DenisNata, 106cl Javier Brosch, 107br (dog) WilleeCole Photography, 107br (mat) RTimages, 108 tl Artem Bilyk, 110 tl Mat Hayward, 110br rebeccaashworth, 112-113 Eric Isselee, 114 bl Javier Brosch, 115tl Monkey Business Images, 115br Eric Isselee, 116bl Eric Isselee, 118tr Richard Peterson, 119tr Eric Gevaert, 119b NatUlrich, 120tr Andrew Burgess, 120bl Mackey Creations

Warren Photographic
88br, 91tr, 91bl, 96br (x2), 97tr (x2), 98bl, 99tl, 99br (x2), 100r (x3), 101t (x3), 101c, 102-103c (x5), 103tl, 103br, 104c (x2), 105t (x2), 105b, 106r (x3), 107l (x3), 108c (x3), 109 (x4)